18th & 19th CENTURY WORKS

THOEMMES

Printed in Great Britain by
Antony Rowe Ltd, Chippenham, Wiltshire

A DISSERTATION ON MATTER AND SPIRIT

John Jackson

With a new Introduction by
John W. Yolton

THOEMMES PRESS

© Thoemmes Press 1994

Published in 1994 by

Thoemmes Press
85 Park Street
Bristol BS1 5PJ
England

ISBN 1 85506 325 5

This is a reprint of the 1735 Edition

Publisher's Note

INTRODUCTION

John Jackson (1686–1763) was the author of some thirty-five pamphlets, mostly to do with theological issues. He wrote to defend the role of reason in religion. He also wrote on human liberty against Anthony Collins, on the existence and unity of God against William Law, and he published a number of defences of Samuel Clarke.[1] The DNB entry (written by the Rev. Alexander Gordon) says that 'apart from his relation to Clarke, Jackson's polemical tracts possess little importance'. Gordon goes on the characterize Jackson as 'a pertinacious writer, without originality or breadth of culture'. Gordon's characterization is in general correct, but we should not overlook the importance of Jackson's tracts as representative of some of the major controversies in the first half of the eighteenth century, especially those on human action, the attributes of God, and that fascinating debate over thinking matter enflamed by Locke to which Jackson's pamphlet reprinted here made a curious and significant contribution.

The standard metaphysical view in the seventeenth century was that of two substances, a material, extended substance and an immaterial, unextended substance. Each of these had its own set of properties which could not be transferred to or shared with the

---

[1] For some discussion of Jackson's writings supporting Clarke, see James P. Ferguson, *The Philosophy of Dr Samuel Clarke and Its Critics* (1974).

other. The immaterial substances, which were the souls of finite creatures (man) were said to be simple, indivisible and immortal. Material substances, matter and body, were divisible, destructible, and, most important of all, incapable of initiating motion. Unlike immaterial substance, matter is not self-active.

When Newton wrote about forces of attraction and repulsion, he was careful to say those forces were not essential to matter, since, were they essential, matter would be active, rather than, as the standard view said, dumb, inert, and passive. Most writers on religion, and most scientists (including Newton) identified God as the only genuine cause, as the only being who could initiate motion and change.

One of the fundamental questions confronting those who worked with this two-substance ontology was, can the two substances (mind and body) interact, can the movement of particles of matter that strike our sense organs cause ideas or thoughts in the mind? Even those who seemed to accept a causal theory of perception confessed that they did not understand how matter could influence the mind. Many were driven to deny causal influence of body on mind, leaving the obvious correspondence between awareness and physiology to God's planning. The more extreme ontologists, Malebranche and his followers, even denied that we move our body: God sees to it that when I will to move my arm, the arm moves. Andrew Baxter, against whom Jackson writes in the *Dissertation*, was just such a strong follower of Malebranche.

The possibility that, as Locke suggested, God might add the property of thought to some systems of matter (*eg*. the brain) would have eliminated the need for immaterial substance: one substance, matter, would then have both kinds of properties, thought and extension. Matter would also become active, at least to the extent that thought (especially in some of its forms, *eg.* willing) was seen as active, as an initiator of action. Thus, Locke's suggestion seemed to his contemporaries to violate traditional doctrines on two counts: it made matter active and it dispensed with the second substance. The debate that swirled around Locke's suggestion of thinking matter spread throughout eighteenth-century Britain. Not many writers took up that suggestion, but a few did attempt to explore the relation between immateriality and immortality, and one or two writers defended the possibility of organized matter having properties not possessed by its parts. Collins was one such writer, engaging clarke on this last point, Toland was another who, in his *Letters to Serena* (1704), says that matter is active. There were a few others who favoured some aspects of the suggestion. It was a complex and pervasive controversy.[2]

Baxter's *An Enquiry into the Nature of the Human Soul* (1733) was a sustained, informed and detailed defence of the traditional metaphysics, with a good dose of Malebranchian occasionalism thrown in. He launched a vigorous attack against the possibility of matter having the property (or power) of thought. The *Enquiry* went through three editions between 1733 and 1745; it attracted much attention. Joseph Priestley later in the century wrote against it. The fact that Jackson attacked certain features of Baxter's *Enquiry* three years after its first appearance indicates that he was informed

---

[2] For the details on this controversy, see John W. Yolton, *Thinking Matter. Materialism in Eighteenth-Century Britain* (1984). .

about the debates around the thinking matter suggestion. Jackson was, as might be expected of a clergyman and Rector of Rossington in Yorkshire, in agreement with Baxter that '*Matter* and *Spirit* are *essentially* different; and have different *Substratas* or *internal Substances*' (p. 42), but he repeatedly qualifies this claim with phrases such as 'so far as we know of them from their Properties' (p. 41). His interest was, he says, in showing that the dogmatic claims made by Baxter for the immateriality of the soul and the essential difference of the two substances are not derived from demonstrative arguments; hence, they are only conjectures or beliefs. But the lengths Jackson goes to support this claim, the amount of detail and cogent argument on the other side, makes one wonder just where his sympathies lay.

His Preface does present the issue clearly in terms of our being compounded of two parts, one intelligent and active, the other unintelligent and passive. The question is, how do these two components differ: essentially or only accidentally, modally? He also characterizes as atheists those who say every being is material, having both properties of motion and intelligence. But Jackson also asserts that those who argue that there is an essential difference between the two substances and that, even the power of God cannot make thought a property of matter, go beyond what our knowledge permits. Even more, Jackson characterizes as 'weak Bigots' those who defend this essential difference and say that if the soul was material, the natural immortality of the soul would be denied. Neither philosophy nor religion teaches that the soul is *naturally* immortal. God's power can make the soul immortal, whether it is material or immaterial.

The *Dissertation* itself goes on, much as Locke had, to argue that our knowledge of substance does not enable us to say what is or is not essential to it. Our knowledge is limited to properties, it does not extend to the internal structures. As many writers did, including immaterialists, Jackson asserts boldly that 'nothing can exist without *Extension* or [without] existing *in space*' (p. 3). He coupled this claim with the equally accepted principle that 'no Existence can be without a *Place* of Existence, or existing *somewhere*'. Place and space too are extended. He of course did not mean to say space or souls were *materially* extended. He, unlike most of those who used this notion of extension, made it clear that extension does not need solidity. Motion also does not apply solely to solid bodies.

With these clear claims, claims that in Locke and others were condemned as materialist-inclined, Jackson proceeds with a convincing series of arguments against various contentions made by Baxter, assertions that Baxter offered in refutation of materialism. The *Dissertation* thus becomes a rather special pamphlet in this heated materialist-immaterialist debate, a clear-headed understanding of the suggestion Locke made about the limitations of our knowledge, the compatibility of thought and extension, even material extension, and the rejection of immateriality being necessary for immortality.

John W. Yolton
Rutger's University
New Jersey
1994

A

DISSERTATION

O N

Matter *and* Spirit :

W I T H

Some REMARKS on a Book,

Entitled,

An Enquiry into the Nature of the humane Soul.

By *JOHN JACKSON,*

RECTOR of *Roffington* in the County of *York,* and Master of *Wigston's* Hospital in *Leicester.*

L O N D O N:

Printed for J. NOON, at the *White Hart,* in *Cheapside,* near *Mercers Chapel.*
M. DCC. XXXV.

[Price One Shilling.]

PREFACE.

T**HE** Subject of the following Dissertation being of no small Importance both in Philosophy and Religion, ought to be freely enquir'd into and seriously attended to. An impartial Enquiry into the Nature of our Souls and Bodies, or of Matter and Spirit, cannot but tend to give us just Notions of the Frame and Constitution of our Beings, to attain which is highly worthy the Study and Endeavours of every rational humane Person.

As we are compounded of two Parts or Beings, one of which is intelligent and active; and the other unintelligent and passive; the great Question hereupon hath been amongst inquisitive men, how far and in what respects these differ from each other : whether they differ Essentially, or in their Original internal Nature or Substance; or whether their Difference only consists in Mode of Existence and some Properties which are not Essential to them,

They

They who suppose every *Being* (*as well as the* humane Soul) *to be* Material, *or* Body, *do in Consequence make Matter* neceſſarily-exiſtent, eternal, infinite, *and also* neceſſarily *endued with* Motion *and* Intelligence: *which is prodigiouſly* unphiloſophical, *and downright* Atheiſm. *The* Mutability *of Matter, which also by Philoſophical Experiments is found to be* finite *and to fill but a very ſmall Part of the* immenſe Space, *is directly repugnant to its ſuppos'd* neceſſary *Exiſtence and* Infinity: *and as all* Motion *is inconſiſtent with abſolute* Infinity *of Being, ſo neceſſarily-exiſtent* Motion (*or even a Conatus to it) neceſſarily deſtroys itſelf*; *becauſe, if* neceſſary *at all, it muſt be neceſſary* every way equally always, *which is contradictory and impoſſible*; *it muſt likewiſe be neceſſary in every Part of Matter and in every Degree of Motion, which is contrary to Fact*; *and wou'd thereby (if poſſible ſo to exiſt) be inconſiſtent not only with a ſtate of* Reſt *in any one Body or Piece of Matter, but alſo with the Compoſition and Formation of Bodies at all, and make the Univerſe a Maſs only of diſunited Atoms. Beſides the* Vis inertiæ *or natural* Inactivity *and* Reſiſtance *of all Matter to* Motion *ſhews demonſtratively that it is not eſſentially endued with Motion, or the Motion of it neceſſarily-exiſtent. And farther both the different Degrees of* Intelligence *in Beings, and alſo the evident Abſence of it in many Beings, in all* mutable, compounded *Matter, demonſtratively ſhew again, that Matter, if at all, is not* eſſen-
iially

tially *or* neceſſarily *intelligent : becauſe, if it was, not only every Part of Matter or diſtinct Material Body wou'd be* equally intelligent ; *but intelligent alſo in every poſſible or higheſt Degree of Intelligence.* So that *it follows from the* Mutability, Finiteneſs *and* Inactivity *of Matter, and the* Variety *of its* Compoſition, Form *and* Motion, *and the* different Degrees *of Intelligence with which Beings are endued, that Matter or Body is not and cannot be* ſelf-exiſtent *and* univerſal Nature : *but it hence demonſtratively follows on the contrary, that there exiſts diſtinct from and independent of Matter and all intelligent finite Beings,* a neceſſarily-exiſtent, eternal, infinite *and* intelligent free Cauſe *or* Agent, *who is the Author of* Matter, *and* Motion, *and of all thoſe* intelligent Beings ; *and who is Himſelf alone neceſſarily intelligent and all-perfect, and the Creator, Preſerver and Governour of Univerſal Nature.*

On the other hand, they who contend that there is a Difference of Nature *and* Eſſential *Properties between* Material *and* Spiritual *Subſtance; and that Matter is incapable (even by the Power of God) of the Property of* Intelligence, *and* Spirit *of the Property of* Solidity, *ſeem to me, for Want of ſufficient Evidence of the Truth of their Aſſertion* [Solidity *and* Thinking *not being incompatible, that we know of*] *to attribute too much to their own Underſtanding, and too little to the divine Power. Wou'd they be contented with a Probability of their Opinion, it might reaſonably be admitted; but Demonſtra-*
tion

tion of it is more than they are able to make out.

Others go farther and alledge that it is derogatory to Religion *to suppose the* Substance *of the humane* Soul *material; that the* Consequence *of it is to deny the* Natural Immortality *of it; and to make it mortal and corruptible like the compounded* Bodily Part *and common* Matter: *and so to take away the* Natural *Proof of a future State, and of* Rewards *and* Punishments, *in another* Life *after this.*

But these can only be the Sentiments of weak Bigots, *who neither understand* Philosophy *nor* Religion; *neither of which teaches that the humane* Soul *(whether material or not) is naturally immortal. And as* Philosophy *informs us, that* Matter *of itself no more tends to* Annihilation *than* Spirit *does; and that probably* Solid *uncompounded* Bodies, *or the original constituent* Parts of Material Beings *are as immutable and incorruptible, as spiritual or intelligent* Substance *is or can be; so both* Philosophy *and* Religion *agree to assure us, that whether the* Soul *is in its own* Nature *mortal and corruptible, or immortal and incorruptible, the* Power *and* Providence *of* God *can and will make it to subsist in a future State, and render it capable of those* Rewards *and* Punishments *hereafter, which are the just* natural Consequence *or the* reveal'd Recompence *of* Good *and* Evil *done in this Life.*

So that if the humane Soul *cou'd be prov'd to be* Material, *that wou'd have no ill Influence on* Religion, *or in the least weaken the natural or*

re-

reveal'd Evidence of a future State. But as on the one hand, some Atheistical Writers, the Cartesians *and* Spinozists, *have given to Matter Powers and Properties that cannot possibly belong to it, and have even deify'd it; so others, thro' a Superstitious Blindness, and Ignorance in Philosophy, have run into the contrary Extreme, and have vilify'd it in an unreasonable manner: tho' they cannot but be sensible of the wonderful and beneficial Powers and Effects of it manifested in the Works of Creation and Providence; and that it is by God's Will and Appointment made the Instrument and Means of all our Knowledge and Happiness here, and, as is probable, also hereafter.* ‖

I thought it proper to premise briefly so much, in order to obviate and prevent any Prejudice or wrong Conceptions which otherwise might possess the Minds of some Readers of the following

‖ I have taken no notice of a new Hypothesis in Philosophy, which hath been lately advanc'd, *viz.* that there is no such Thing really existing in Nature as *Substance*, either *Material* or *Spiritual*; and that what is so call'd is only an Aggregate of *Properties* without any existent *Subject :* so that *Extension, Solidity, Intelligence,* &c. exist without any Thing or Being *extended, solid, intelligent,* &c. In Consequence of this Philosophy it follows that there is *Motion,* but no *Mover* or Thing *mov'd; Life,* but no Thing *living; Agency,* but no *Agent; Virtue,* but no *Virtuous Person; Sin, but no Sinner;* divine Attributes and Perfection, but no perfect *Being* or *God.* This is a Scheme of Philosophy so wholly unsupported by any Reason or Evidence, and so contrary to the common Sense of Mankind, as well as to that of the greatest, Philosophers, and is withal so visionary and unintelligible, that the ridiculous Absurdity of it (if no ill Consequences attended it) must render it incapable of a serious Confutation.

Differ-

Diſſertation on a curious and difficult Subject; and which is written with that impartial Freedom which ought eſpecially to be allow'd and encourag'd in all Matters of Philoſophy *and* Religion, *which are the only Ornaments and Perfection of every rational Nature.*

A

A

DISSERTATION

ON

Matter and *Spirit*.

IT is on all hands granted without controversy, that we know nothing of the *internal Nature, Essence* or *Substance* either of *Matter* or of *Spirit*; or what that internal *Constituent* or *Substratum* is, which is the *Ground, Foundation* or *Subject* of the *Properties* existing in them. The Reason of this our Ignorance is, that it is not the Object of any of our *Senses*; nor can be discover'd by any *reflex* Act of our Minds either upon Matter or upon themselves.: and therefore the Reason we call the one *Matter*, and the other *not Matter* or *Spirit*, is not deduc'd from our Knowledge of their *internal Substances*, but of their *external* different *Properties* only, which we know cannot exist without a Subject. Hence it follows that we cannot certainly know [unless there was an apparent essential Contradiction between them] whether the *different Properties* we

B   ob-

obferve in them, and which is all we know of their *Difference*, and from which we are apt to conclude their internal Effences and Subftances to be *different* in Kind or Species, are really *effential* (and fo incompatible) or not ; or fuch as that the Exiftence of their internal Subftance or Subftratum depends upon them ; or without which it cou'd not be what it is.

I prefume we do not know, and therefore cannot fay of a Certainty, but that the *Subject* or Foundation of the Properties either of Matter or Spirit may poffibly exift abftract from or without the *different* Properties we ever yet obferv'd in them, and by which we properly diftinguifh them : and therefore in confequence we cannot be certain but that the *Subftance* of Matter and Spirit may be the *fame* ; and that they differ only by fuch different Properties or Modes of Exiftence or Powers of exciting Ideas in us [not fuch as are *Effential* to either, but fuch] as it is the *Will* of God for different Ends to inveft them with.

From what is faid it clearly follows, that we cannot know that *Matter* cannot *think* ; or that *Spirit* may not be *meerly paffive* and *folid* ; that is, whether the *Subftance* or *Subftratum* of what we call *Matter* is not in any refpect or under any poffible Mode of Exiftence capable [by the Will and Power of God] of *Confcioufnefs* and *Intelligence* ; and the *Subftance* of what we call *Spirit* is not in like manner capable of *Solidity* and *mere Paffivenefs* : and therefore that their Difference with refpect to our Knowledge of them

them is not *effential* or *internal*, but only *no-minal* and *external*. I mention *Solidity* and *mere Paffivenefs* in *Matter* in oppofition to *active Intelligence*, and fomething fuppos'd to belong to *Spirit*, for which I want a proper Name, in oppofition to *Solidity* (I will for the prefent call it *Non-refiftence*) becaufe I am apt to think that when Things are rightly confider'd, thefe are the only Differences we with reafon conceive to be between them; and by which we moft properly diftinguifh them.

Some indeed have thought *Extenfion, Figure* and *Mobility* peculiar to *Matter*; but till fome better Reafons be given for this Opinion than I have hitherto met with, I fhall conclude that nothing can exift without *Extenfion*, or exifting *in fpace* [and Extenfion certainly may be without *Solidity*, they being as different Ideas as any two whatever, nor any way inferring reciprocal Coexiftence, and fo Extenfion cannot be peculiar to Matter] for no Exiftence can be without a *Place* of Exiftence, or exifting *fomewhere*; and no *Place* can be without Extenfion or Space, Place being evidently only a partial Idea of Extenfion or Space: and Spirit exifts and acts *in Space*, as evidently as Matter exifts and is acted upon by it *in Space*; and therefore is and cannot but be extended as Matter is. The actual Exiftence of an *unextended* Point, or fomething really exifting, and yet not exifting *in Space*, is not only impoffible and unconceiveable; but fuppofing Spirit or thinking Subftance to be fuch, it cou'd not receive Objects at once from more

B 2 Points

(4)

Points than *one*, or from any real Extenſion, and
ſo cou'd not perceive anyThing *extended:* which
is contrary to Experience.

Secondly ; whatever is *finitely* extended muſt
have an external Termination of Exiſtence, and
ſo have *Figure* ; and for the ſame Reaſon it muſt
be alſo capable of *Motion* ; as we every day ſee
in Fact that *Spirit* is, (ſuppoſing our Souls to be
ſuch) being mov'd with the Body ; but if by
Mobility be meant the motion of internal parts,
then Spirit is not indeed capable of ſuch a Motion (that we know of) nor *ſimple, ſolid* material Subſtances (which Only I conſider in this
Argument) neither.

This being laid down, there are ſeveral Arguments and Objections to be anſwer'd.

Firſt ; 'tis ſaid that *Matter* is *eſſentially ſeparable* and *Spirit eſſentially inſeparable* and *indiviſible:* Secondly,that theProperty of *Intelligence*
or *Conſciouſneſs* is an *individual* Property of the
whole thinkingSubſtance,but that there is *no individual* Property of the *whole*Subſtance of Matter :
and therefore, 'tis argued, their internal *Eſſen-
ces* and *Subſtances* cannot be the *ſame.* Theſe
two Arguments or Objections depend on each
other ; for I ſuppoſe the beſt Reaſon any one can
give why the Soul is *indiviſible* (its not being
extended being a mere Fiction and plain Abſur-
dity) is becauſe *Conſciouſneſs,* a Property of it, is
not *diviſible* in Idea into more or ſeveral *Conſciouſneſſes.*

Granting this *Indiviſibility* of Spirit or thinking Subſtance [which yet is more than we certainly know, tho' probable] it does by no means
prove

prove the internal Substance or abstract Substratum of *Matter* and *Spirit* to be different [the only true Question being, whether the Properties of the one are compatible to the other;] but only that *Spirit* is a *simple,* and *Matter* (so far as it comes under our Notion and Knowledge) a *compound* Being: that is, strictly speaking, Matter is not *one* Substance, but many *simple* Substances united together by mutual *Attraction* or *Gravitation* and *Cohesion,* [which Powers, whether they belong at all to intelligent Beings, we know not:] and it is for this reason only that *Matter* is truly said to be *divisible,* and thence infer'd to be incapable of an *individual* Property belonging to its *whole* Substance, as being compounded of *simple* parts *separable* and actually *separated* from each other ; and so is not *one* Substance, but a Mass of Substances; the Original *simple* parts of which *compound* Substance, and which are in themselves distinct Substances, are as *indivisible* as the Substance of *Spirit*; and equally capable (for ought we know) of the *individual* Property of *Consciousness* or *Intelligence.* For individual *Consciousness,* &c. does not exclude or is inconsistent with the *Extension* of the *conscious* or *intelligent* Being ; or is a *Consciousness* arising from something which is absolutely divested of all Physical Parts ; nor as being an *unextended* Property infers the Substance or Substratum of it to be also *unextended,* any more than the *unextended* Properties of Matter, *Solidity, Inactivity, Mobility,* &c. infer Matter it self to be *unextended*; but it is the Property of a Being whofe parts are one *Continuum*, and fo peculiarly *connected*, that the *whole* is at once *uniformly* affected; and fo every *Action* or *Paffion* is not of a *Part*, but of the *whole* Subftance; and in this fenfe *individual*: tho' in ftrict metaphyfical Reality the Affection of *one Part* cannot be the *individual* Affection of *another Part*; or the *Perceptivity* of one Part the *individual Perceptivity* of another Part; any more than the *Exiftence*, *Solidity* or *Mobility* of *one Part* of any continued, *fimple corporeal* Subftance, can be the *individual Exiftence*, *Solidity* or *Mobility* of *another Part*. The only Queftion therefore again is, whether *Matter* is capable of that *Mode* of Exiftence, or that particular *Connection*, in which the Property of *Intelligence* or *Thinking* feems to confift.

That the *Original fimple Subftances* of which *compound* Matter is form'd, are or may be of an *individual* and *infeparable* Nature (for which Reafon I am apt to think all *Spirits* or *cogitative* Beings, however they may differ in Extenfion, are of an *individual*, *infeparable* Nature) may thus be clearly prov'd, *viz.* It muft be granted that God can create the *leaft* Particle of Matter, or *leaft* material Body or Subftance which is capable of exifting: but it is evident from what has been before argued, or rather it is *felf-evident* that the leaft or all material Subftance cannot but be *extended*; and therefore there may be *extended material* Subftance abfolutely incapable of *Divifion*, or of an abfolute *infeparable* Nature. For to fuppofe it to have a

fepa-

feparable Exiftence, when it is the *leaft* Subftance capable of exifting, is a direct Contradiction : becaufe a fuppofition of its being *feparable* and exifting in a *feparate* ftate, is a
fuppofition of its *not* being the *leaft* fubftance,
when it is fuppos'd to be the *leaft*. Therefore
the *minute, original, fimple* Parts of *compound*
Matter, or fimple, material Subftances which
are the *leaft* that are capable of Exifting, muft
be *folid* and as *indivifible* as *Spirit* or *thinking*
Subftance can be fuppos'd to be ; and the Properties of them of one uniform Nature : and
fo, notwithftanding the foregoing Objections,
the internal Subftance or Subftratum of *Matter*
is (for ought we know) as capable of *Confcioufnefs* or *Intelligence*, as that of *Spirit* is ; and
may be the fame *fpecific* Subftance. When
in the preceding Argument, I fay, the *leaft
Particle of Matter*, or *the leaft material Subftance or Body* ; this is to be taken only as
a Suppofition (which cannot with any Reafon be difallow'd) that God can exert all
the Power that relates to the Production of
Beings ; (for a Power which cannot be exerted,
is no Power at all :) and hence it will appear
to be an Abfurdity to fuppofe that there is or
can be in Nature a Piece of Matter exifting in
a *fingular, fimple*, or *uncompounded* ftate, which
is *lefs* than that which God can produce.
Whence I infer, that tho' in Nature there can
be no fuch thing as the *leaft* Particle of Matter,
fince all muft have Extenfion and Parts, there
may neverthelefs be Matter or Body produc'd
by

by God, which is *essentially indivisible*, as being
the *least* (tho' extended) which Power can produce, or which can exist in a *singular state*, as
an *entire, individual, uncompounded* Existent.
So that the Substance of unthinking Matter
cannot be *always* (perhaps the original, solid
Particles of which compound Bodies consist
are not at all) *actually divisible*, any more than intelligent Substance is. Notwithstanding I wou'd
not affirm that God's Power in the Production
of *thinking* Substances (any more than in the
Production of *unintelligent* Substance) is by the
Nature of the things confin'd to a particular
Extension ; but it seems to me not to be absurd
to suppose that he may *encrease* or *diminish* the
Extension of the Existence of any *thinking*
Being : and that, if there is any such Thing
as a different Species of intelligent created
Beings, their different Natures may depend
on something that we know nothing of,
and not on their having each particular Kind a
particular individual Extension *essential* to them.
From what is argued, I wou'd farther observe, that if it be possible for Matter to
be *intelligent*, the *thinking* Faculty probably
cannot depend on any particular *Extension* ; but
on a particular *Connection* or *Union*, and particular *Impulses*, and *Impressions* altogether un-
known to us : and as Body or Matter may
be (for ought we know) capable of these, so
it will be very hard, if not impossible, to prove
that the Property of *individual Consciousness* may
not or does not exist in *material* Substance.

It

It is not a sufficient proof of it, that Matter has Properties which are not individual Properties of the *whole* Substance; for so hath intelligent Substance likewise. As there may exist and be conceiv'd in the same Body at the same Time, different Figures distinct from that particular *individual* Figure of the *whole*, which is necessarily form'd by the Termination of its extreme Parts; so the same may exist and be conceiv'd in the Soul likewise; as being only the necessary Consequence of Finiteness of *Extension* in both: *Motion* also, which may be various and difform in the same Being at the same Time, is no more an individual Property in *intelligent* than in solid unintelligent Substance: and the Motion of a *simple*, *solid* (or even of a *compound*) Body in a straight Line is but *one individual* Motion of the *whole* Body; just as it is in the like Motion of Spirit: and *Duration* is as much an *individual* Property of the *whole* Substance of Matter, as either that or *Consciousness* is of the *whole* Substance of *Spirit*. So that *individual* or *indivisible* Properties of the *whole* Substance, which are common both to Body and Spirit, neither prove *Spiritual* Substance to be absolutely *indivisible*, nor to be *Essentially* different from *Material* Substance. This Point will be farther consider'd presently. In the mean time it is, I think, sufficiently prov'd, that as whatever exists, is *extended* more or less, or exists in more or less space, whether in a *solid* and *resisting*, or in an *unsolid* and *unresisting* manner; so it is no Con-

C   sequence,

sequence, that whatever is *extended*, muſt have
Parts actually diviſible. The words *Parts* and
diviſible are us'd ambiguouſly. When we ſay
a Thing conſiſts of *Parts* and is *diviſible*, we
mean Parts not of *ſimple* but of *compound* Subſtances; we ſpeak of *Things*, not of *one Thing*; of an
Union of Subſtances which are not only *ſeparable*
but *actually ſeparated* in Exiſtence for want of
Connexion, let the *Extenſion* be what it will.
But *that* hath no Parts in this Way of Speaking,
which is *one ſimple* Subſtance perfectly *continued*
and *connected* without *Vacuity*, let the Extenſion alſo be more or leſs, and the Subſtance
ſolid or not. And all ſuch *ſimple uncompounded*
Subſtances, as I take the *original*, *ſolid* Particles of Matter to conſiſt of, tho' neceſſarily
extended, are probably not *actually diviſible* by
any external natural Force or finite Power:
but whether the Power of God the Creator
himſelf cannot diminiſh the Extenſion of any
ſimple Subſtance (material or immaterial) which
has not the *leaſt* poſſible Extenſion, without
deſtroying its Exiſtence, or changing the Eſſential Properties of it, is a Thing, I preſume,
above the Reach of our imperfect Knowledge
to determine with Certainty, as I obſerv'd before: only it ſeems moſt probable to think that
his Power may either add to or diminiſh at
pleaſure their Exiſtence without Annihilation
of them; there being no aſſignable Reaſon to
conclude that all ſimple material or Immaterial Subſtances ſhou'd be of the ſame finite
Extent, or the *leaſt* which are capable of Exiſting.

ifting. But yet I believe it is true in Fact,
that all *folid* or perfectly *continued* Subftances,
or the original, minute fimple Particles or
Conftituents of compound Bodies are indivifible by all thofe *natural* Powers or Forces which
are apt to divide and feparate the Parts of *compounded, difcontinued* Subftances.

From what is juft now faid it will appear
that another Argument alledg'd to prove that
the *Subftance* of Matter and Spirit is not the
fame, has no Weight in it: viz. that *Matter* is
of a *mortal* and *corruptible* Nature, and *Spirit*
of an *immortal* and *incorruptible* Nature, and
therefore, 'tis argued, they cannot be of the
fame Nature, Effence or *Subftance* ; and that, if
they were the *fame*, Spirit wou'd be naturally
mortal or *corruptible*, as we fee all Matter is.
This Argument is already obviated ; and is
built on the falfe fuppofition that all Matter
confifts of *naturally feparable* Parts, and therefore muft be *naturally corruptible :* all Corruption of it being nothing but the Alteration of
the Form and Qualities of *compound* Matter,
by actual *Separation* or different *Cohæfion* of its
Parts, occafion'd by external Force or internal
Motion ; whereby external Parts flying off from
the whole Mafs, or the Cohæfion of external or
internal Parts being quite broken or alter'd, the
Body puts on a new and different Form and
has different Qualities from what it had before.
This Corruptibility therefore plainly relates only
to Matter confider'd as a *Compound* Being, of
which the *fimple, folid, original* Parts are not

(fo

(fo far as we know) naturally capable; and
therefore Matter in its *fimple, uncompounded*
Nature is as *incorruptible* and *immortal* as
Spirit can be with Reafon fuppos'd to be ;
nor is more fubject to *Separation* or *Diffolution*
of its Frame than Spirit is. But there is another
fenfe in which the Soul may be confider'd
either as being naturally mortal or immortal,
diftinct from the Corruptibility or Diffolution
of its Subftance, *viz.* as it is confider'd either
in a ftate of Union with Body, or as exifting
without fuch Union. For if Union with Matter or Body is neceffary to preferve the *Intelligence* and *Agency* (which are the proper Life)
of the Soul; this Union being *diffolv'd*, the
Soul muft be in a ftate of Mortality and Death,
tho' the Subftance of it fhou'd continue *un-
diffolv'd*. This is a Point which, I think,
Philofophy cannot demonftrate one way or
other ; and fhall be confider'd farther hereafter.

An ingenious and learned Author, in a late
Book entitled *an Enquiry into the Nature of
the humane Soul*, has undertaken to demonftrate
the *Immateriality* of intelligent acting Subftance,
which we call *Soul* or *Spirit*, and the Impoffibility of *Matter* or *Body* being intelligent and
active, by feveral Arguments which I fhall
carefully confider. Firft, he argues againft the
poffibility of Matter being endued with *active*
Power, from the *Solidity* of it, after this manner : * " *Matter* as a *folid* Subftance necef-
" farily

* **Enquiry into the Nature** *of the humane Soul.* p. 84.

" farily refifts all Change of ftate ; therefore
" it is incapable of being endued with that
" Power that could change its ftate : if it was
" capable of being endued with this Power, we
" fhou'd be oblig'd to deny its Refiftence ; and
" therefore its Moment, as alfo its folid Exten-
" fion. In fhort, it is as incapable of being
" the Subject in which this Power and Refift-
" ence can at once refide, as of being the Sub-
" ject in which Refiftence and its contrary can
" at once refide. *Matter* therefore is incapable
" of all Kind of *Activity*, or of being endued
" with any Power, except that one negative
" Power of remaining in the ftate in which it
" at prefent is. "

The Import and Force of this Argument, I
think, amounts to this, *viz.* that what is or can
be confider'd as *unactive* and *refifting* Motion,
cannot by any Faculty or Power infus'd into it,
become *active* and *felf-motive* ; or be conceiv'd
to have in it a Capacity of *Life* and *Activity* ;
becaufe Refiftence to Motion and Inactivity, and
Life, Self-motion and Activity are contrary to
each other. To which it may be anfwer'd,
that this Argument proves nothing by proving
(as we fhall fee) too much. For if the *Soul*
(let the Subftance of it be what it will) is not
originally endued with *innate* Ideas, or the
Perception of Ideas is not *effential* to it, it muft
be conceiv'd, before its Perception of *Ideas* by
Senfation or Reflection (which is a change of
its ftate caus'd by means of Matter) to be an *unactive* Subftance, without any innate Power of
chang-

changing its ſtate ; and endued only with a Capacity of *Life* and *Activity*. This muſt be its Condition before its Union with Body, or before its Reception of Ideas. So that this ingenious Author muſt plead for innate Ideas as eſſential to the Soul, which can never be prov'd, and ſeems highly improbable to be Fact ; otherwiſe the Soul without Ideas muſt be allow'd to be as *dead, inert* or *unactive,* as the Body is without *vital Motion :* and ſo, if it can have in it a Capacity of *Life* and *Activity* directly contrary to its primary ſtate of *Unintelligence* and *Inactivity,* which ſeems to be common to it with Matter ; it may notwithſtanding this Author's Argument be *material.* And farther, ſince this Capacity of Life and Activity is excited and exerted in the Soul by Means of *Matter,* or by the Impreſſion of Matter upon it ; it may hence ſeem more probable that it is material than not. Experience aſſures us that the Soul never thinks without the Help of Matter : in reflecting on its own Ideas, which is an Act of the Soul moſt of all independent of Body, 'tis evident that it acts or reflects not without the Help of the Body or animal Spirits ; as every one us'd to think intenſely muſt know by the Laſſitude and Pain often occaſion'd thereby : the denying * this is a plain Error in our Author. Therefore the *Soul* is *chang'd* by the Action or Impreſſion of Matter upon it from a ſtate of *Inſenſibility* to a ſtate of *Senſibility,* as *Matter* is *chang'd* by the Impulſe of Matter from a ſtate of *Reſt* to a
ſtate

* *Enquiry,* p. 223. in a Note.

ftate of *Motion*: and as the one has always a Faculty or Capacity of receiving and retaining *Ideas*, fo the other has of receiving and retaining *Motion*: but it follows not hence that the Soul is neceffarily always percipient or has Ideas becaufe capable of having them, any more than that Matter is neceffarily always in motion, becaufe it is capable of it. It is true that Matter cannot *move* and *reft* at the fame Time or in the fame refpect; nor can the Soul perceive and not perceive Ideas, or act and not act at the fame Time. Contrary Powers or Capacities may refide in the one and in the other; as a Power of *moving* and alfo of *refifting* Motion, or a Power of *reft*; a Power of *Acting* or of not acting; a Power of receiving or not receiving or hindering the Reception of Ideas: tho' thefe contrary Powers cannot be exerted or have Effect at once or in the fame refpect, in the one or in the other. Where then is the Abfurdity of fuppofing two contrary Powers in the fame Subject; the *Pofitive* Power of *felf-motion* or *acting*, and the contrary *negative* Power of *not acting* or *moving*, or of refifting Motion? Suppofing indeed thefe two Powers to be *Pofitive* and *Equal*, it wou'd be a manifeft Abfurdity for the fame Subftance to be endued with them; but if we fuppofe the felf-motive or *active* Power always fuperior to the Power of *refifting* Motion or Action, both Powers may be compatible and refide in the fame Subject: Juft as we fee in Matter two directly contrary Powers continually ope-

operating; one in the *Gravitation* of it, another in the *Cohæsion* of its Parts always *resisting* and counteracting the *Gravitation*. A Particle of Air, for Example, by one Power constantly gravitates towards the Earth, and by a contrary Power of Repulsion flees from it, and keeps its parts cohæring : and it is the same in all Bodies which are not fluid, or are not horizontal. And this ingenious Author himself has shewn and well explain'd these contrary Powers in Matter. † And if it is no Absurdity for an external Agent (which I admit with this Author to be the cause of these contrary Powers in Matter) to act thus contrarily at once upon Matter, for good and wise Ends; and Matter is susceptive of or passive to two contrary Powers at once; it can, I think, be no Absurdity to suppose contrary Powers to be lodg'd *in* Matter it self. What Matter is capable of receiving passively or from an *external* Mover, it may be capable of receiving from Powers *within* it self. *External* Power impresses contrary Affections or Tendencies at once in Matter, why may not *internal* Power in Matter it self do the same? So that there appears not any Absurdity in supposing that by the Power and Will of God Matter may move itself ; or have a self-motive or acting Power within its Nature capable of overcoming by the Faculty, we call *Will*, or by its *Agency*, the *Essential* Resistence, which as a *solid* Substance it always makes to Motion, or when in Motion, unto Rest ; *i. e.* may have an internal Power of changing its own State. And there seems

to

† *Enquiry*, P. 63, 64. in Not.

to be no Difference in the Cafe, whether the
acting felf-motive Power be *in* material Subftance, or be fo united *to it*, as in Fact it is, that
the Body continually acts upon it, and refifts
the active Power exerted in every corporeal
Motion. So that there are in Fact thefe very
two *contrary* Powers, which our Author thinks
fo great an Abfurdity to be together, *united* and
continually *counteracting* each other. And I
do not perceive the Confequence, that, if
Matter was capable of being endued with a
Power of changing its ftate, or of Self-motion,
we fhould be oblig'd to deny its *Refiftance*, and
folid Extenfion. When Matter is mov'd by an
external Force, its Refiftance to *Motion* is over-
come, and a Power of continuing in a contrary
State, *viz*. of Motion, and its Refiftance to
Reft is equal to its Power of continuing in a
ftate of Reft and of refifting Motion : and yet
it retains its Moment and folid Extenfion and
Refiftance to Motion, as before it mov'd ; either
with refpect to refifting the Motion of other
Bodies, or any Encreafe or Diminution of its
own Motion. So here are two contrary Powers at once in Matter confiftent with its folid
Extenfion ; the Power of refifting *Motion*, and
the Power of moving or refifting *Reft* : it refifts
a Change of its State to *Reft*, and at the fame
Time refifts *Motion* or a Change of its State to
more or lefs Motion. Its Refiftance is to *contrary* States at once, but not in the fame Refpect ; for any Degree of *Motion* is contrary
to a State of *Reft*. Juft fo, fuppofing the Soul

a folid extended Subſtance, this living Subſtance by its *Solidity*, (in which reſpect it is *paſſive*) reſiſts the Self-motion or Action of the
Will upon it ; and whilſt it is ſelf-mov'd, ſtill
retains its property of being at Reſt, or reſiſting Motion ; and reſts when the *Will* acts
not upon it or moves it not : as dead Matter
when mov'd by an external Force ſtill retains
its reſiſting Power, and reſts when any Force
overcomes its Motion, as it moves when any
Power overcomes its Reſiſtance to Motion, and
its Property to reſt. The Conſiſtency of theſe
contrary Powers is, that they are not *equal*; and
the internal ſelf-motive Power or Agency,
which is a *poſitive* Property of the Soul, is always ſuperior to its *Negative* Power not to
move or act ; as external Power is always ſuperior to the *vis inertiæ* of Matter, or its Reſiſtance to Motion.

In Truth, abſtract from *Life* and *Agency*, e-
very Subſtance equally has what our Author
calls *the Negative Power of remaining in its
preſent State* ; ſo far the *vis inertiæ* is common
to all Subſtance as ſuch ; and it may be ſaid to
reſiſt a Change of its State, becauſe its State
cannot be chang'd without ſome external or internal Power apply'd, which is ſufficient to
change it. So that if (according to our Author's Arguing) an intrinſic Principle or active
Power which can change its State is incompatible with this negative Reſiſtance to a Change
of it, no Subſtance can be capable of *Life* or
Agency : and ſolid Extenſion, if any Thing
diſtinct from this *vis inertiæ*, or *negative* reſiſting

fisting Power to a Change of State, has nothing
to do in the Argument.

But Secondly; suppofing a f -motive Power in Matter to be inconfistent w h Refistance to
Motion, or with its *folid* Ext fion ; no Abfurdity will hence follow, fo ng as it is not
inconfistent with Extenfion bfolutely : the
thinking or felf-motive Subf nce may ftill be
the fame with that of M tter, tho' it be
not *folidly extended* ; it ay have (for
ought we know) Extenfi without *Solidity*, thefe being different Idea, and in no
wife inferring each other. Vhether it be proper to call Substance *Mat *, which hath no
Solidity, may perhaps be a uestion : but Solidity, not being Effential t extended Substance,
let us fuppofe the Substan e of Soul to be extended *unrefisting* Substan , and confider whether any Abfurdity will llow. This Author
refers, to fhew the Abfurdities of this Suppofition, to N°. 22. *Sect*. 1. and N°. 26. All that is
infifted on in thefe Places is,

    1*ft*, That Matter, if *refisting*, cannot have
two contrary Conatus's implanted in it; in Proof
of which he refers to N°. 14, 15. This has been
already confider'd, and fhewn to hold only where
the contrary *Conatus's* are equal : and this Author himfelf has fhewn that contrary Conatus's
not equal may be and are implanted in Matter,
or imprefs'd upon it, in the univerfal Cafes of
Gravitation and *Cohæfion* of all Bodies, efpecially
which are *perpendicular* or not *horizontal* to the
Centre of Gravity ; and Air, in every Pofition
of it, conftantly tends to the Centre of Gravity

by

by the Power of Gravitation imprefs'd upon
it, and alfo conftantly flees from it by its
Elafticity or repulfive Power.

2*dly*, Our Author argues; *if it is unrefifting
Matter it could never move other Matter, unlefs
that other Matter cou'd be mov'd by Nothing at
all.* For proof of this he refers to N°. 21.
wherein it is only prov'd that Matter, where
no *Life* or *Agency* is in it, moves other Matter
and is mov'd by it by their Powers of mutual
Refiftance and Contact; and we cannot conceive how dead unintelligent or unactive Matter fhou'd move other fuch Matter without
them. But if *Contact*, the *vis inertiæ* or *folid
Refiftance* is neceffary to *move Matter*, then
that will exclude all *unrefifting* Subftance, as
well as *unrefifting* Matter, from being a Mover
of Matter ; which is both abfurd in itfelf, and
alfo, in contradiction to what this Author in-
tended to prove, infers that the Soul cannot
move the Body, or any Part of it, or be mov'd
by it, becaufe its Subftance is *unrefifting* and
incapable of *Contact*, and of the Action of the
Body upon it. But if Body can act upon the
Soul (fuppos'd to be unrefifting Subftance)
without Contact or mutual folid Refiftance ;
why may not the Soul (tho' unrefifting Subftance) act upon the Body without Contact,
or mutual folid Refiftance ? So that if the Author's Argument here proves any Thing, it
proves quite too much; and fuppofes the Subftance of the Soul (be it what it will) if *unrefifting*, not to be able to act upon or to move
Mat-

Matter, if nothing can act upon it or move it but what is *folid* or *refifting*. By his Argument, the Soul by its felf-motive Power may move its own Subftance, but cannot move Matter, becaufe unrefifting, any more than unrefifting Matter can move other Matter. But if, as he fuppofes, ‡ contrary to his Argument alledg'd here, that *unrefifting* Subftance can move *refifting* Subftance or Matter; why not *material* unrefifting Subftance as well as *immaterial* unrefifting Subftance? Put the Faculty call'd *Will* or *Agency* into Subftance without *Solidity*, then this *unrefifting* Subftance [which may be *material*, unlefs it can be prov'd that *folid Refiftance* is effential to Matter, and that the Subftance of Matter cannot exift without it] will move Matter juft as the Soul does by its fubftantial Prefence and Power of acting: Contact or not Contact, refifting or not refifting having, I think, plainly nothing to do in the Agency or in *moving Matter*. Thus this Author's Argument is anfwer'd; which indeed entirely depends upon begging the Queftion, and fuppofing that Matter cannot act upon or move Matter, if you take from it its folid Refiftance, and do not give it felf-motive Power or Agency inftead of it: but does not prove that without *folid Refiftance* it cannot move Matter by an *active* Power, or that it is not capable of an active Power. A felf-motive or active Power in an *unrefifting* Subftance will move Matter, he muft ‖ own;

fo

‡ *Enquiry*, p. 87. Sect. 31.   ‖ *Enquiry*, p. 87. Sect. 31.

fo that nothing depends upon the Subftance
being *refifting* or *unrefifting* ; but the whole
depends on the Poffibility or Impoffibility of
Material Subftance, whether refifting or not
refifting, being by the Power of God invefted
with *Agency* or *Activity* or a *felf-moving
Power*. If he cou'd fhew that it is of the
Effence of Matter as Matter to be *folid* and
refifting ; then he muft fhew next (to fhew that
Matter cannot think) that *Solidity* or *Refiftance*
to *Motion,* is incompatible with *thinking* or
Agency : which Part of the Argument has been
confider'd ; and it hath been made appear, I
think, that they are not incompatible. But
it proves nothing by fhewing only that Matter
without *Solidity* and *Agency* too cannot *move
Matter* ; if it can have Agency (which is the
Point in Queftion) it can move Matter, tho'
its Subftance be *unfolid* or *unrefifting,* nothing
is more evident. Befides, to fhew farther the
Confiftency of *folid Refiftance* with *active Power*,
it may be obferv'd, that *folid Refiftance* is not
contrary to *Agency,* but to *Motion,* which is
not *Agency,* or *vice verfa* : So that tho' it may
be contrary to a *felf-motive* Power, it is not
contrary to an *active* Power. We know not
that the Soul *moves it-felf* in its Agency ; or
is ever mov'd, but by and with the Body,
which is mov'd in Concurrence with the *Will*
of the Soul, partly by its Agency and alfo by
Powers which perhaps we know nothing of.
So that for ought which appears yet to the
contrary, the Soul may have both *folid Refi-*
ftance

(23)

stance and *Agency*, without *Self-motion* ; or *Self-motion* and *Agency* without *solid Resistance* ; or even *Self-motion*, *Agency* and *solid Resistance* all together.

Another Argument against the *Materiality* of the Soul, from which also this ingenious Author infers the natural *Immortality* of it, is that it hath no *Extension* or *Parts*. If this cou'd be prov'd, it wou'd, I confess, prove it to be *not material* ; but then it wou'd not prove it to be *positively immaterial,* or a positive acting Substance, *not material* ; but it wou'd prove it to have no Being or Existence at all. Existing Substance without Extension is as inconceivable, as Existence without Existence ; *Space* or *Extension* being necessary to the Existence of all real Beings or Substances.

His Argument is this * : " The Parts of ac-
" tive, perceptive Substance, if it [the Soul] cou'd
" have any, must be also active and perceptive,
" from this Consideration, that to suppose it
" otherwise, is to allow that Activity and Per-
" ceptivity may result from the joining toge-
" ther dead inert Parts ; which is the same Con-
" tradiction whether we allow it in material or
" immaterial Substance : for it is to make the
" Effect perfecter than the Cause, by supposing
" Perceptivity and Spontaneity both of Mo-
" tion and Thought, and Reason itself to arise
" from the mere Addition or Junction of
" Things dead and inert to other Things e-
" qually dead and inert. " ——— " Thus a liv-
" ing

* *Enquiry,* c. 3. *Sect.* 9, 10. p. 105, 106.

" ing Subſtance made up of dead Parts is a Con-
" tradiction; and a living Subſtance made up of
" living Parts, is not *one* living Subſtance, but as
" *many* diſtinct living Subſtances, as there are diſ-
" tinct living Parts in it. And indeed this *Compo-*
" *ſition* and *Diviſibility* of living Subſtance muſt
" infer the ſame Conſequences, as if we ſuppos'd
" Matter a thinking living Subſtance : the ſame
" Multiplicity or rather infinite Variety of
" Conſciouſneſs and Perception muſt be as well
" in the one Caſe as in the other. But this is
" falſe, as plainly appears from the *Simplicity*
" of our Conſciouſneſs and Perception——And
" from hence it follows, that Parts and Divi-
" ſibility are not Affections conſiſtent with
" active perceptive Subſtance, which muſt be
" *one* and *ſimple* without Compoſition. *Di-*
" *viſibility* is ſuch an Affection of Subſtance as
" ſhews on the one hand, that *Matter,* becauſe
" *diviſible,* cannot think or be a living Sub-
" ſtance ; and on the other, that ſpiritual Sub-
" ſtance, becauſe *thinking,* cannot be *diviſible*
" or have Parts."

This Argument againſt the *Extenſion* and
Materiality of thinking Subſtance conſiſts of two
Parts; one, of a ſuppos'd Contradiction of dead
inert Subſtance being by any means made living
and active Subſtance ; the other Part ſuppoſes
that a perceptive Subſtance having Extenſion
and Parts muſt be *diviſible,* and cannot be *one*
individual ſimple thinking Subſtance, but many
diſtinct thinking Subſtances, and conſiſt of as
many diſtinct Conſciouſneſſes as of Parts.

To

To the firſt Part of the Argument it may be reply'd; what is *dead, inert* Subſtance? It can only mean in the preſent Argument, Subſtance not endued with *actual Thought* and *Conſciouſneſs,* and an *actual ſelf-moving Power.* I ask therefore what is the Subſtance of the Soul (in this Author's Senſe) before it has any Ideas implanted in it, or before it is join'd to Matter, and receives Impreſſions from it? can it exiſt without Ideas or Conjunction with Matter or not? If it can exiſt without Ideas (as he muſt own it can, unleſs he holds Ideas *innate* and *eſſential* to Spiritual Subſtance) it is then, and till it receives Ideas, what he calls *dead, inert Subſtance,* with only a *Capacity* of receiving Ideas, and exerting Self-motion concomitant with its Ideas, and occaſion'd by them. It is like a *tabula raſa,* not written upon, but capable of receiving Characters. And where's the Contradiction? It is in a ſtate of Inactivity, but capable of Activity: as a Body at *Reſt,* which is capable of *Motion,* cannot move without a Mover; ſo neither can the Soul become ſelf-motive or active, till it is acted upon by the Impulſe of Matter or ſome Agent. There may be ſome particular *Connection,* beſides mere Union, in the Parts of thinking Subſtance, on which its Capacity of thinking and acting depends. Nor is this making the Effect perfecter than the Cauſe; becauſe thinking and acting is ſuppos'd to be the Effect of a Power or Faculty within the Subſtance itſelf, but which cannot be exerted without the Union and Impreſſion of Matter, or ſome external Agent, acting upon it.

E   Is

Is it not as marvellous that mere dead, inert and unactive Matter fhou'd have Power to *excite Ideas* in the Soul, and be the Materials of *Senfation* and *Knowledge*, as that Matter fhou'd be fo form'd by an Almighty Power, as to be able to *receive Ideas* from material Impreffions, and to retain them, and to act and be felf-motive by Reflection on them ? fo that this Part of the Argument has no Weight in it. And if he had fuppos'd the Soul to be originally endued with Ideas (which Notion I hope he will not defend) it wou'd not ftill appear impoffible for *material* Subftance to be originally endued with innate Ideas, any more than for *that* or any *other* Subftance to be capable of receiving them by means of corporeal Impreffions.

Our Author fometimes diftinguifheth between *Acting* and *Activity*, *Perception* and *Perceptivity*; as if he thought the *Activity* and *Perceptivity* only were *effential* and *infeparable* Powers of the Soul; but then at other times he infifts that *thinking* and *acting*, or the *Exercife* of the Powers of Activity and Perceptivity is no lefs *effential* and *infeparable*; which is abfurd on any Suppofition but the Soul being endued Originally with innate Ideas, that Ideas are *effential* to and *infeparable* from the Soul. But in a feeming Oppofition to this, he fays; " * The " humane Soul is indeed at firft without *Knowledge* " *ledge* and without *Experience*, but hath the " *Power* of attaining both." How can it be *without Knowledge and Experience*, if *thinking* and

* *Enquiry*, p. 168.

and *acting* are, as he says after, *essential* and *inseparable* in it ? This is a Contradiction. The Reason then why the Soul is at first *without Knowledge* plainly is, because it is without *Ideas*, which are the materials of *Knowledge*; and therefore because *thinking* and *acting* are not *essential* and *inseparable* in it : And what is the Soul *without Ideas*, without *thinking* and *acting*, but *inert, unactive, senseless* Substance ; and why may not such a Substance be *material?* The *Power* of *Perception* or of Life and Action is no more *Life* and *Acting*, than the *Power* of seeing is *seeing*; or than the *Power* of receiving *Motion* or any particular *Figure*, is really and actually *Motion* or any particular *Figure*. What then is this Power of Perception and Action, which, if the Soul receives, at least it exerciseth it not, till it is united to Body ? and Matter is certainly the *Instrument* of its Exertion, tho' not the *Efficient Cause* of it. The Power undoubtedly is implanted in it by God, and whether *material* Substance is capable of it or not, remains to be prov'd. If we had never experienc'd *Motion*, perhaps we might have thought *Motion* as incompatible to *Matter*, as we think *Perception* and *Action* to be. I suppose that our ingenious Author will not contend for *innate* Ideas of the Soul, or that it is *Essential* to it always to think ; tho', as observ'd, he says that thinking is *essential* and *inseparable* in it : and if this cou'd be prov'd, the *Immateriality* of the Soul wou'd be prov'd beyond all Dispute. But on the contrary to this, he explains his own meaning of the

E 2   na-

natural *Activity* and *Perceptivity* of the Soul ;
which, fays he, * " can only properly be meant
" a *Power of acting*, and a *Capacity of per-*
" *ceiving* ; and by being *active* and *perceptive*
" is meant the *Exercife* of thefe Powers, or *real*
" *Action* or *Perception:* " yet as forgetting what
he had almoft juft faid, he very inconfiftently
† fuppofes, that the *Activity* and *Perceptivity*, or
the *Capacity* of acting and perceiving is the fame
as *real* Action and Perception ; at leaft that the
letter is as *Effential* to and *infeparable* from the
Soul, and as *independent* of Matter, as the other.
For to the Objection, viz. ‖ " It is allow'd
" that the Soul hath *Activity* or *Power* in it-
" felf, but at the fame time cannot *exercife*
" this Power or put forth any *Act*, unlefs
" it be united to the Body ; or that the Body
" gives it Occafion to act and exert its Power ;
" and fince it cannot act without this Occa-
" fion given it, that therefore it depends on
" being united to the Matter of the Body, as
" a Condition, *fine qua non*, tho' not as an
" *Efficient Caufe* in exerting any Act : " To
" this Objection he replies ; ‡ " firft, he fays,
" it is an exprefs Contradiction that an *active*
" Being fhou'd depend on a *dead* Subftance
" for the exerting its Activity ; fo that it
" cannot put forth any Act without it is firft
" acted upon by that *dead* Subftance : all
" Action muft certainly fpring out of its
" own Nature." Is not this pleading for the
abfolute Independency of the Soul upon the
Body

* *Enquiry*, p. 111.   † Ibid. p. 121.   ‖ Ibid.   ‡ Ibid.

Body with refpect to its receiving by the Action
or Impreffion of Matter upon it any Ideas,
which are the Inftruments of the Soul's acting:
and therefore unlefs he had meant what is here
faid only of the Soul in a feparate ftate after
its Difunion from the Body, he muft mean
that Ideas are *Effentially* inherent in the Soul;
that it is Originally and by its Nature actually percipient; and that the Union of it with
Body does not *promote, advance* or *forward*
the active Power it is endued with, but on
the contrary, *limits, reftrains* or *hinders* its
Activity; fo that had our Souls never been
united to Bodies, they wou'd, he muft conclude, have been more *knowing* and *active*
than with them. And that this is his meaning, his immediate following Words declare. ‡
" It [the Soul's Activity] may indeed de-
" pend upon the dead Subftance, fo far as
" that *limits, reftrains* or *hinders* its Activity;
" and this is the Way that dead Matter
" really affects the Soul in their prefent U-
" nion; the Power of the Soul is *limited*
" and *confin'd* to a certain Manner of Action and
" Degree of that Manner; and the Matter of
" the Body is neceffary to its acting in this
" confin'd Manner and Degree; but this very
" Confideration fhews us that its *native* Power
" wou'd be more *unconfin'd,* if fuch Impediment
" and Limitation were taken off; and I affert
" that no man can conceive it poffible that
" the Soul fhou'd depend upon dead Matter for
" *pro-*

‡ Ibid.

" *promoting,* *advancing* or *forwarding* the active
" Power it is endued with."

This reasoning is too important to be admitted without clear Proof of the Truth of it, which is impossible to be had. It looks as if he held a preexistent State of the Soul to the Body; and that by way of Punishment the Soul is confin'd to the Body as to a Jayl, wherein its Original preexistent or innate Ideas are limited or hinder'd from being exerted into actual Knowledge and Agency, farther than the Clog of Matter to which it is confin'd will permit it to exert its *Native* Perception and Agency. If this is not his meaning, what he says has no Argument in it against the Objection propos'd by himself to be answer'd : and if it is his meaning, and if the Impression of Matter upon the sensitive Organs does not convey Ideas into the Soul, and thereby *promote,* *advance* and *forward* the percipient and active Power with which it is endued, he must (against all Philosophy and Experience) account for our Ideas and Knowledge some other Way independent of Matter ; and of which we have not any Idea or Consciousness or Perception. He must shew why we never reflect on Ideas, but such only as were convey'd thro' the Bodily Organs, if the Soul has other Original Ideas independent of the Body, or of any Ideas which were convey'd by dead Matter : and if our Knowledge and Action spring from the Nature of the Soul itself without the Help of Matter, and so far as Matter does not hinder it from springing
out,

out, our Author muſt ſhew why an Infant
whoſe ſenſitive bodily Organs are vigorous
and no way obſtructed, is not as percipient
and actually knowing as the wiſeſt Man or
greateſt Philoſopher. If Matter does nothing
but *hinder* the Original Faculties from exerting
themſelves, without furniſhing any Materials
for *Perception* and *Action*, the Original innate Knowledge of the Soul wou'd ſhew itſelf or be exerted at once and in every degree,
ſo far as Matter wou'd permit it ever to be
exerted. This is plain ; and therefore on the
contrary to this Author's reaſoning I think,
that the Soul is of ſuch a Nature as requires an
Union with Matter to furniſh it with Ideas,
and ſo to enable it to exert its percipient and
active Powers ; and never thinks or acts without
it. Without theſe Ideas the Soul cou'd not
perceive ; and without *Perception,* the active
Power cou'd not be exerted ; and the Soul
wou'd have no Ideas (that we know of) if it
was not united to Matter, and receiv'd them
thro' or by means of its material Organs.
And he is quite miſtaken in ſaying that the
Soul || " in reflecting upon its own Percep-
" tions even in this ſtate of Union, does not
" reflect with the help of the Body, as an
" Inſtrument to perform ſuch an Action."
'Tis certain the Soul no more *reflects* than it
perceives without the help of the Animal Spirits and Organs ; it may as well ſpeak without
a *Tongue,* or move the Body without *Muſcles*
and

|| *Enquiry,* p. 123.

and *Limbs:* And the Act it exerts upon the Body or Spirits in *reflecting*, or *moving* any of the Parts of it, is not *prævious* (as he thinks) but only *concomitant*, as other Impulses and Motions are. So the *Immateriality* of the Soul is not yet prov'd.

Let us now confider the Second Part of our Author's Argument, *viz.* that a perceptive, active Substance having *Extension* or *Parts*, must be *divisible*, and cannot be *one, simple, individual* acting Substance, but *many* distinct Substances; and must confift of as many distinct *Consciousnesses* as of *Parts.* To this it may be reply'd ; that the *Simplicity* of Thought and Consciousness is not sufficient to prove the Soul to be *unextended* and *indivisible*, because this at least is as confiftent and conceiveable with a Connection of *Parts* and *Extension*, as without them. When Matter *impels* Matter, the *Impulse, Force,* mutual *Resistance* and *Action*, is but *one simple Impulse,* &c. tho' made by many extended Parts or material Substances mutually impelling, refifting and acting upon others. The *Impulse* of one Body striking another is but *one simple* Impulse, and is so conceiv'd. A single *Vibration* of an *Elastic* Body, or the *Pulse* of an *Artery* of the *Heart*, is but *one simple Vibration* and *Pulse,* tho' many Particles of *extended* Matter concur in the forming it. The *Motion* of a moving Body is but *one simple Motion* ; and the *Figure* of a Body is but *one simple* Figure of the *whole* Body: so that *Simplicity* of Properties and Affections is confiftent

fiftent with *Extenfion* and *Parts*. Suppofing
the Soul or thinking Subftance to be *one Continuum*, or Connection of Parts without Vacuity, it is reafonable to think that every Senfation and Confcioufnefs fhou'd be *one fimple* Affection ; tho' every Part concurs or is affected
in the Senfation or Confcioufnefs : the *Simplicity* of *Thinking* and *Confcioufnefs* may be the
Refult of the Soul's being inftantaneoufly affected in every Impreffion from *without*, or Vo-
lition from *within* ; as when a folid Body impels another, their mutual *Momentum* is the
inftantaneous Refult of *every Part* of each of the
Bodies *acting* and *reacting* ; and the Momentum of each of the whole Bodies is but *one
fimple individual Power*. As there may be
Connections and Union of Parts that we know
nothing of, fo *fimple individual* Confcioufnefs
or Perception may be the Effect or Refult of
fome particular Connection, which makes
Subftances which are *extended* as much *one*, as if
they had *no Extenfion*, if that was poffible.
And it is full as wonderful and difficult to conceive that a Multiplicity of folid extended Parts
of Matter, by their Impreffion on the Soul,
fhou'd excite but *one fimple* Senfation or Perception, and not as many as there are Parts of
Matter acting, or as different Bodies would do,
as that every Senfation or Perception of the
Soul confifting of *continued* Parts fhould be
one and *fimple*. But as the Reafon of the
one I fuppofe to be, that the *Medium* of every
Senfation or Perception confifting of almoft in-

F   finitely

finitely fmall Particles which compofe the animal Spirits, and their Impreffion or Action
being uniform and inftantaneous, makes their
Impulfe on the Soul to be *one fimple* perceptible
Impulfe; fo in like manner, tho' every Part of
the Soul be affected by every material Impulfe,
the entire Continuation and Connection of the
Parts of its Subftance, the whole of which is
uniformly and inftantaneoufly affected, make the
Effect to be *one fimple* or *individual* Perception.
But according to our Author's reafoning, Matter in order to excite a *fimple* Perception in
the Soul fhou'd be itfelf *unextended*, as well
as the Soul be fo, in order to have a *fimple*
Perception excited in it: there is as much Reafon one way as the other.

I know not why this Author fhou'd conclude from the Suppofition of the *Extenfion* of
thinking Subftance, that it muft be *compounded*
and *divifible* into many diftinct thinking Subftances: if nothing is *one fimple* Subftance but
what has no Extenfion, then we can have no
Idea of *one fimple* Body or material Subftance,
nor can any fuch exift, becaufe Matter is men-
tally divifible *in infinitum* and always extended.
But on the contrary, I take all perfectly folid
Body to be *one fimple* Body: and fuppofe a
folid Body exifting, which is the *leaft* capable
of exifting, or the *leaft* which God can create,
it muft by the Terms be abfolutely *one* and
indivifible, tho' *extended*: and the Connection
of the Parts of thinking Subftance (tho' material) may be fuch as that a Divifibility of them,
(which

(which may not be in the power of any finite Agent) may deſtroy its Nature and
thinking Properties.

But it is a ſtrange Notion of *Unity* of Subſtance, that nothing can be *one ſimple* Being,
but that which is *nothing*. For to have no *Extenſion* or Exiſtence *in Space*, is to exiſt *no where*,
or *not at all*. *Soul* as well as *Body* hath evidently place of Exiſtence; the Soul moves from
one place to another as well as the Body; nor
can any more act in two Parts of Space or in
two Places at once than the Body can : and to be
in Place and to change Place denotes *Extenſion*,
of which *Place* is only a partial Idea. Nothing
is more ſelf-evident than that thinking Subſtance acts *in Space*, otherwiſe it acts not upon
Body, which is falſe : if it acts *in Space* or upon *Body* exiſting *in Space*, it exiſts *in Space*, and
poſſeſſes Space by its Exiſtence ; elſe he muſt
ſay it exiſts and acts *where it is not*, which he
knows to be abſurd, and has rightly obſerv'd
(P. 29.) " Nothing can act *where it is not*.
" This is one of the plaineſt, moſt unexcepti-
" onable Principles. To ſay a Thing *acts* and
" yet is not *where* it acts, is to ſay nothing
" acts there." Thus thinking Subſtance acts
in Space or *Extenſion*; but if itſelf exiſts not *in*
Space or is not *extended*, it either acts and not
acts, or acts where it is not ; that is, it acts *in*
Space and yet is not *in Space* ; is *preſent* to and
with *extended* Body and acts upon it, and yet is
preſent to no Part of Body, becauſe every Part is
extended, if it is not it ſelf *extended*. All which

F 2   are

are manifeſt Abſurdities and Contradictions.
The Concluſion therefore is ; that as the *neceſſarily-exiſtent* acting Subſtance of God fills all
Space with its Preſence, and ſo can act *every
where* ; and does act in the whole Creation by
an univerſal Providence ; and his Sphere of Action is as large as the *infinite Space* itſelf ; ſo
every created thinking and acting Subſtance has
a Sphere of Action in ſome Part of Space to
which it is preſent, and in which it exiſts, and
acts only where it is preſent, not by mere *Virtue*
or *Power* without *Subſtance*, which is abſurd
[becauſe *Power* cannot be or be *conceiv'd* to be
without *Subſtance*, or where *Subſtance* is not]
but by *Virtue* or *Power* exiſting in *Subſtance* or
a real Subject, and exerted only where the Subſtance *is*, not where it *is not*.

Our ingenious Author has one Argument
more to prove the *Immateriality* of the Soul,
which deſerves to be conſider'd. He thus argues ; † " Since it hath been ſhewn that *Mat-
" ter* is a dead Subſtance in all reſpects, it fol-
" lows that the *immaterial* Subſtance or the
" Soul is the only Thing in us that hath active
" Power. And ſince it hath active Power,
" that Power muſt inhere in it as in its Sub-
" ject ; or the Power muſt belong to the Soul
" as a Property of its Nature—and ſince active
" Power muſt belong to the Soul as a Property
" of its Nature, that Property cannot be ſepa-
" rated from it, *without deſtroying its Nature
" altogether* —— thus active Power cou'd no
" more be ſeparated from the Soul without an
　　　　　　　　　　　　　　　　　　　　" Act

† *Enquiry,* p. 113. Sect. 3.

" Act of Omnipotence to deſtroy its Nature,
" than *Solidity* or *Inactivity* cou'd be ſeparated
" from Matter, without an Act of Omnipo-
" tence to deſtroy the Nature of Matter.——
" This, I ſay, is abſolutely neceſſary, otherwiſe
" we ſhou'd make Activity and Power *a mere*
" *Accident in Nature,* which is prodigiouſly
" abſurd. "

Anſw. To make Activity of thinking Subſtance *a mere Accident,* I grant to be abſurd ; becauſe it is plainly *permanent* ; and is not the Reſult of any known *Matter* and *Motion.* Its
Nature alſo may depend probably on the particular Connection and Frame of its Subject, and
may be deſtroy'd upon a Diſſolution or Alteration of that Connection : So the bodily Organs
depend on a particular Frame and Connection
of their Parts to enable them to act and convey
Senſation and Ideas to the Soul, and their Nature and Powers wou'd be deſtroy'd upon a
Diſſolution or Alteration of their Frame. The
Powers of theſe material Organs are not *mere*
Accidents, but Original Qualities inherent in
them ; and yet I ſuppoſe no body doubts but
that the *Subſtance* of theſe Organs might and
wou'd exiſt without theſe Qualities, and that
they might be ſeparated from it : ſo in like
manner (for ought we know) the Connection
and Frame of the Soul, on which the active
Power of it depends, may be diſſolv'd or chang'd,
and the Power thereby be ſeparated from it,
without deſtroying the *Subſtance* in which this
Power inheres ; and that by another Conſtitution
of it the ſame Subſtance may be made altogether
paſſive

paſſive and *unintelligent.* If *Active Power* was as *eſſential* to the Soul, as *Figure, Mobility* and *Extenſion* are to *finite* Matter [we know not that *Solidity* is equally eſſential] this wou'd be a ſufficient Demonſtration of the *Immateriality* of the Soul; becauſe we ſee that all Matter has not this Activity, if any at all, in its preſent State and Mode of Exiſtence, is capable of it ; of which we know nothing likewiſe : but if it was an *eſſential* Property, it muſt belong, if to Matter at all, to all Matter equally and univerſally, as the other eſſential Properties do. But there does not appear to me the ſame immediate and neceſſary Connection between the *Power of Acting* and the *Exiſtence* of the *Subſtance* in which this Power inheres ; as there does between the *Exiſtence* and the *Extenſion, Mobility,* &c. of *Matter.* And as there may be a Conſtitution and Connection of *material* Subſtance that we know nothing of, ſo I think we cannot know, and that this Learned Author has not demonſtrated but that the Power of thinking and acting may poſſibly be the reſult of ſome particular Conſtitution of *Matter.* That nothing like Thought or active Power reſults from Matter and Motion, that we have Experience of, is no wonder ; becauſe we may as ſoon by Matter and Motion form a *thinking* Subſtance, as any one of the material *Organs* of Senſation : ſo no Argument can be drawn from our Knowledge of the Powers of *Matter,* to conclude certainly thereby that it *is* or *is not* capable of Thought and active Power.

All

All the Confequences which our Author has deduc'd from his Notion of thinking Subftance, as ftrongly follow from the *Materiality* and *Extenfion*, as from the *Immateriality* and *Inextenfion* of it : Matter in its own Nature or by the *Will* of God being as capable of *Incorruption* and *Immortality*, as any other created Subftance can be fuppos'd to be. And fince the *Scripture-Revelation* fo much magnifies the Power of Matter, as to amplify the future Reward of virtuous and good Men with the Promife of giving them a *glorious* and *incorruptible Body*, form'd in the Likenefs of our Saviour's *heavenly* Body ; we ought in Reafon to conclude that *Matter* is not of a contemptible Nature, but is capable of being a fit Companion for the Soul, and of promoting its Happinefs in a State of the greateft Perfection which the Soul is capable of.

Our ingenious Author labours hard to anfwer this Argument in behalf of the Excellency and great *Perfection* of Matter : He owns that it may be fo *refin'd*, as to be a *lefs Impediment* to the Soul than it is in the prefent ftate ; but ftill, he thinks, it is but *dead, inert* Matter : and if, as he infifts, it cannot *help* the Soul in any of its Perceptions and Operations, but even when *refin'd*, is an *Impedimemt* to it, *limits* and *confines* it ; and that the Soul is more *unlimited* and *active* without it ; no Account can be given, why the Soul after Death or in the future ftate fhou'd be *reunited* to a Body, and that very Body of *dead inert Matter* be join'd to it as a

Reward

Reward given to it, and for the Confummation of the Soul's Felicity: Since, according to this Author's Notion of the Soul and of Matter, the Soul was in a more perfect ftate before this Reunion with Body, the bringing it out of a *better* ftate to reward it with a *worfe* is ftrangely abfurd to be fuppos'd. This Confideration therefore makes it more than probable (and it is moft agreeable to Philofophy and reveal'd Religion to think) that the Soul is in an *imperfect* ftate without Body; and can no more exercife its Faculties of Perception and acting without it, than an Artift can exert his Skill without Inftruments; and the better and more perfect the Inftruments are, the better and more perfect is his Work. This is the moft rational Notion of the Soul's Condition both here and hereafter.

I fhall make no Apology for the foregoing Remarks on the excellent Book of our ingenious Author; becaufe I am perfuaded, that as a Philofopher and Lover of Truth he will not be difpleas'd with them : nor do they at all derogate from the Force of the main Defign of his Work, which is to confute *Atheifm* by a Demonftration of the *univerfal* Providence of an Omnipotent and All-wife Agent diftinct from, and independent of *Matter*, and who is the *Creator, Preferver* and *Director* of it. This Argument he hath handled with great Judgment and Learning; and has fo demonftratively confuted the Scheme of *Atheifm*, that his Book
is

is highly worthy the ferious and careful perufal of all Lovers of Truth and Religion.

Having confider'd carefully and impartially the Nature of *Matter* and *Spirit* (fo far as we know of them from their Properties) and the principal Arguments which have been alledg'd for the *Immateriality* of the Soul, and to prove that the Subftance of Matter cannot be the fame with the Subftance of Spirit, or be capable of Thought and active Power, and fhewn that thefe Arguments are not *demonftrative* ; I think I may from what hath been argued on both fides of the Queftion build the following Conclufions on very good Reafon.

Firft, If the *Subftratum* or internal Subftance of *Matter* and *Spirit* be the *fame*, then the Property of *Intelligence* or *Agency* belongs only to *fimple* Matter, divefted of all *Compofition* of *feparated* and naturally *feparable* Parts, and perhaps of the Property of *Solidity* or *Refiftance :* and Secondly; the *fimple* material Subftance invefted with this *thinking, acting* Property, never by any Power of *Gravitation, Attraction* or *Cohæfion*, or any other Way of Union, becomes *compounded*, as *unintelligent, paffive* Matter is ; but that, as the latter is always an *Heap* or *Mafs* of Subftances difunited and without entire folid Connection, fo the former always continues *fimple* and *uncompounded :* and very probably (tho' we cannot be abfolutely certain) there never was or is an Aggregate of *Perfons* or *intelligent Agents* ; or more Perfons than *one* exifting in *Subftantial Union* ; as we obferve daily many

G   dif-diſtinct Subſtances to be united and mix'd in *compound Matter*. So that I am apt to think it true in Fact, that, whether Matter and Spirit have the ſame ſpecific internal Subſtratum or not ; *active, intelligent* Subſtance is always *ſimple* and *uncompounded*, and not acted on by the Powers of *Gravitation* and *Cohæſion* ; and *paſſive, unintelligent* Subſtance is always *compounded* by the Powers of *Gravitation* and *Cohæſion* ; and that, as there is no ſuch Thing as a perfectly *ſolid, ſimple material* Subſtance or Body exiſting ſeparately by itſelf, without *Cohæſion* with others ; ſo there is no ſuch Thing as an *intelligent* Subſtance exiſting in a *compound* State, or in *Subſtantial* Union and Cohæſion with others. And this Conſideration, that *unintelligent* and *unactive* Subſtance, which we call *Matter*, always (ſo far as we know) exiſts in a *compound* State, inveſted with *Solidity*, and ſubjected to *Gravitation* and *Cohæſion* by which it becomes alſo *mutable* ; and that *intelligent, active* Subſtance, which we call *Spirit*, always (ſo far as we know) exiſts in a *ſimple, uncompounded* State, and not ſubjected to *Gravitation* and *Cohæſion*, whereby it continues *uniform* and *invariable :* This Conſideration, I ſay, ſeems to me as good a Reaſon as can be given to conclude that *Matter* and *Spirit* are *eſſentially* different ; and have different *Subſtratas* or *internal Subſtances* ; it being not probable that the *ſame Specific* Subſtance ſhou'd be inveſted with ſuch different Powers, and have contrary *Modes* of Exiſtence, and not be ſubject to the ſame *natural Laws*. But 3*dly*,

ſup-

suppofing the internal Subftance or Subftratum of what we call Matter and Spirit to be the *fame*, it is not neceffary that *intelligent* Subftance or Spirit fhou'd be invefted with the Property of *Solidity* or *Refiftance*, either to *act* upon other intelligent Subftance or Spirit, or upon *unintelligent Subftance* or *Matter*, or to be *acted upon* by them : and it is highly probable, if not certain, that, tho' *Matter* acts upon *Matter* (fo far as it really acts) by its *folid Refiftance*, or by mutual *impulfive Contact* ; yet it *acts* upon, and is *acted* upon by the *Soul* to which it is united, by fome other Power or Property, and not by *Solidity* ; and that, in confequence, tho' nothing can ever *really act* without being *prefent* where it acts, Spirit may act upon Spirit reciprocally, by being perfectly *prefent* to each other, without mutual *Contact* or *Solidity* ; and even *Matter* may poffibly act upon *Matter* by being *prefent* without *Contact* (tho' we know nothing of any fuch Thing in Fact) fince we have Reafon to think that it acts upon the *Soul*, to which it is united, by being *prefent* to it without *Contact*. And therefore *Solidity* is not (for ought we know) an *effential* Property, or neceffary to the mutual Action, of *Matter*. Hence we may conceive that *Souls* or *Spirits* may have no need of *Material* Vehicles or Bodies in order to act upon each other ; but may act by their own immediate *fimple* Prefence to each other *without* them, as well as *with* them : and it is in itfelf as hard to conceive *how* they act upon each other, thro' a material Medium in a ftate of *Uni-*

on with Body, as without any such Medium and Union. *4thly*; It is highly reasonable to believe, that, whether the Substance of *Matter* and human *Spirit* be the *same* or not; every *simple, material, unintelligent* Substance, and every *simple, intelligent* or *spiritual* humane Substance is perfectly *homogeneous*, or of the same *specific* Nature and *essential* Properties: and that as all the different Powers and Virtues of *compound* Matter arise solely from the different *Motion, Figure* and *Cohæsion* of the *simple solid* Parts of which Bodies are form'd; and might (was our Knowledge of them perfect) be entirely accounted for this way; so also that the different Degrees and Kinds of *Intelligence* in Men derive their sole Original from the different Exercises and Acts of their intelligent Part, consider'd with the different Impression which external Objects thro' a different Disposition of the sensitive Organs make upon the Soul. And perhaps the sole Reason why Brutes differ from each other in Degrees and Kinds of Intelligence, as well as from Men both in *Intelligence* and the entire Want of all *moral* Properties, may be the different Constitution of their bodily Organs, or a different Union of the *intelligent* with the *unintelligent* Substance, [whereby the same Impressions cannot be made in all by the *material* on the *spiritual* Part, or reciprocally on each other] consider'd with the different Exercise of the intelligent Faculty. For we observe not only that some Brutes are more intelligent than others of the same Kind, by a longer Use and Exercise of their intelligent Faculty; and by

Helps

Helps afforded them by Agents of greater Intelligence, *viz.* by Men, for their greater *Ufe*,
Service or *Diverfion* ; as alfo probably by a different Difpofition of the Organical Parts : but
we obferve likewife, that thofe Brutes are moft
intelligent and fagacious, the Formation of
whofe Brains and fenfitive Organs is the likeft
to that of Men.

Hence alfo 'tis not improbable, that the different Degrees of our *intelligent* and *moral* Properties in the *future* ftate from what they are
in *this*, may owe their Foundation to that
Change which our Bodies fhall then undergo,
by which thro' a different Frame and Confti-
tution of Bodily Organs and different Union of
Soul and Body, different Impreffions will be
made by them reciprocally on each other ; and
from thence different Powers and Qualities
arife : the Soul will be enabled to receive objects of Senfe more clearly and vividly, and to
perceive the Reafons and Relations of Ideas
and Things more diftinctly, perfectly and in-
tuitively ; and to act both upon itfelf and the
Body more vigoroufly : which confider'd, with
the *undifturb'd Exercife* of the Faculties of
both without *Intermiffion* upon fuch Objects as
fhall then be prefented to them, may probably lay all the Foundation and be the whole
Caufe of the Perfection of that ftate. And this
is the more probable, becaufe we are inform'd
from *Scripture*, that the *Bodies* of the *Saints*
fhall rife [like Stars of different Luftre and
Brightnefs] with different Degrees of *Glory*,
more or lefs like the *glorious Body* of Chrift

our

our Saviour, according to the different Degrees
of their *Virtues* upon Earth : And the Foundation of the Encrease of Happiness *in the
other World* seems wholly to be laid in the
Addition and *Encrease* of *bodily Perfections*, by
which means the Soul will be plac'd in a more
perfect state, and capable of greater Improve-
ments of all its Faculties. And perhaps our
Saviour's Words (*Joh.* xiv, 2.) *in my Father's
House are many Mansions*, may have a *literal*
Sense, and mean that according to the Degrees of Men's Virtues [who believe in him]
here on Earth ; and also of those who liv'd
well under the *Law*, and in the state of *natural Religion* [for God is *the God and Father
of all*] suitable *Mansions* or Habitations are pro-
vided and fitted to the several Degrees of the
glorify'd Bodies which they shall receive at the
Resurrection : that so all those who shall then
be exalted to an equal state of Happiness shall
have Bodies of an equally glorious Frame,
and cohabit together in the same *Mansion, Re-
gion* or *Climate* [if I may so say] of the *new
Jerusalem* or the *Heavenly state*, which is suited
to the Frame and Constitution of their Bodies ;
all of them enjoying the Presence of Christ
their Head ; and the Communications and
Revelations of the *One God and Father of all,
who is all in all.* And farther, if it be true
[as the Antients unanimously thought] that
all intelligent created Beings were united to
material Vehicles or Bodies in which they
acted ; the different Degrees of their Orders or
Per-

Perfections may have no other Cause than
the different Contexture and Union of their
Bodies with the intelligent Part, whereby they
are dispos'd and enabled to act with different
Power and Efficacy, and to receive different
Influences and Communications of Knowledge
from the Fountain of *divine Revelation.*

These will be thought but *probable Conjectures*; and I do not propose them for *Cer-
tainties*; but freely own, that notwithstanding
what is said, it may be true, that the *Substance*
of *Matter* and *Spirit* is *essentially* different;
and that the Faculty or Capacity of *Intelligence* and *Activity* is *essential* to the *Substance*
or *Substratum* of *Spirit*; and that the *Nature*
or *Substance* of *Matter* is incapable of it. It
may be also true, that not only the intelligent
Part of *Brutes* differs *essentially* from that of
Men, but also the intelligent Part of one Brute
differs from that of another; and even of some
humane Persons from others: and so we may
proceed, not without reason, to infer that the
different Powers and Perfections of *Spirits* or
intelligent Beings in the invisible state may
result from their different Natures and Substances; and that there may be a Progression
of *Species* of *intelligent* Beings, from the *lowest*
to the *highest* Degree of Intelligence; and that
those different Species may by the divine Power
and Will be so fram'd either as not to act
without *material* Vehicles or Bodies, or to act
without them.

But

But whatever is the real Truth and Certainty
of thefe Things, in which our Knowledge is
too imperfect to determine, and Religion is no
way concern'd; I lay it down for a moft un-
doubted Truth, that the *Subftance* of *God* cannot be of the *fame Nature* with *Matter*; nor
can poffibly be of the *fame Species* with any
other *Spirit* or *intelligent Subftance* whatfoever.

1ft; That the *Subftance* of *God* cannot be of
the *fame Nature* with *Matter* is evident; becaufe *Intelligence* is *Effential* and *Neceffarily*
exiftent in the divine Subftance : but if *Matter* is at all capable of Intelligence, yet 'tis
evident that Intelligence is not *effential* or
neceffary to it; if it was, *all Matter* as fuch
muft be not only *intelligent* but *equally* and
in every poffible Degree of *Perfection*, *intelligent*; becaufe *effentially* and *neceffarily* fo :
which is directly contrary to all the *Senfe*,
Reafon and *Experience* of Mankind.

For the fame Reafon God's Subftance cannot be of the fame Nature with any other
Spirit or intelligent Subftance whatfoever; the
Intelligence of all *created* or *deriv'd* Beings
[and fuch all Beings befides God neceffarily
are] being not *effential* or *neceffary*, but ad-
mitting of Degrees according to the *Will* of
Him from whom they are deriv'd.

2dly; The Subftance of *God* cannot be the
fame with *Matter* becaufe it is *Effentially* and
neceffarily infinite or *immenfe*; and by Confequence comprehends and exhaufts all Subftance of its Kind; and therefore [fuppofing

it

it to be *material*] it muſt exclude the Exiſtence of all *other* Matter : ſo that either God is not *material* or elſe no *Matter* exiſts but which is *his Subſtance :* but the *Finiteneſs, Compoſition, Mobility* and *Diviſibility* of *Matter* (as well as *Paſſiveneſs* and Want of *Active Power* and *Intelligence*) ſhew that *Matter* is not *God's Subſtance*, which is *neceſſarily infinite, uncompounded, indiviſible, immutable* and *immoveable* (as well as neceſſarily *active* and *intelligent*.)

For this Reaſon alſo it cannot be the ſame with the Subſtance of any *other Spirit* or *intelligent* Subſtance whatſoever ; for if it was, then that *other* ſpiritual intelligent Subſtance beſides his muſt not exiſt, even whilſt it does exiſt; and muſt be his *individual* Subſtance, even while it is *another*, which is evident Contradiction : and no *deriv'd* Subſtance can be *eſſentially* or *neceſſarily-exiſtent* and *infinite*, that being a direct Contradiction alſo ; becauſe whatever is *deriv'd* can only be ſuch as the *Power* and *Will* of that Being from whom it is deriv'd, makes it to be. 3*dly*; Two *neceſſarily-exiſtent* or *underiv'd* Subſtances [which muſt as being ſuch be *neceſſarily-infinite* in Subſtance and all Perfections] is a direct Contradiction again ; becauſe *one* infinite by containing and exhauſting all the Kind, neceſſarily excludes the Exiſtence of another infinite *homogeneous*.

But 4*thly*; tho' the Subſtance of God is neceſſarily Infinite, and being ſo, muſt neceſſarily be *ſimple, uncompounded* and *ONE* ; and admits

H   of

of no poſſible *compound Union* either with *Mat-*
ter or *Spirit*, or any *particular* Union at all
with either ; but is *eſſentially* and *equally* preſent to all Things, whether of a *ſpiritual* or
material Nature, and by its Exiſtence contains
all of the *ſame Nature* ; yet it does not exclude
the *Exiſtence* and *Preſence* of other Things of
different Subſtances, whether *finite* or *infinite* ;
whether of a *ſolid* and *reſiſting*, or of *unſolid*, *un-*
reſiſting Natures. The *Modes* of the *Preſence*
or *Exiſtence* of *different* Subſtances being ſuppos'd to be *different*, they may coexiſt in the
ſame place, without *coinciding* or being *identi-*
fy'd. *Solid* or *reſiſting* Subſtances (we know) exclude others that are *ſolid* or *reſiſting* ; but we
know not that they exclude thoſe which are
unreſiſting : *Matter* excludes *Matter*, but perhaps not *Spirit* ; and Spirit excludes from its
Place or Preſence all Spirit of the *ſame Kind*, or
which has the ſame Mode of *Exiſtence* and
Preſence, but (poſſibly) not Spirit of *different*
Kind. And therefore (for ought we know)
God and *Matter* and all the Species of *Spirit*
may co-exiſt in the ſame Place by being *preſent*
in different Manners.

What is now ſaid of the *Poſſibility* of *Matter*
and *Spirit*, and of ſpiritual Beings *different* in
Kind exiſting in the ſame Place, which ſuppoſes a Penetration of Dimenſions, I deſire the
Reader to take only *pro hypotheſi*, and for Con-
jecture ; for I do not pretend to know whether
the *Subſtance* of any Spiritual Agent (beſides
God) is *ſolid* and *reſiſting*, or *not ſolid* or *unre-*
ſiſting ;

sifting; and so whether any two Substances (be-
sides God and his Creatures) can be coexistent,
or exist in the same Place.

I shall conclude this Dissertation on *Matter*
and *Spirit* with observing that it is most reasonable to think [according to the unanimous Opinion of the antient *Christian* as well as *Heathen*
Writers] that no Being is purely *immaterial*
but *God*; and that it is most suitable to the
Nature of all created Agents to be *united* to
some Kind of *material* Vehicle or Body, wherein they act and whereby they exert their spiritual Faculties. The Reasons for this Opinion are briefly these following; *viz.*

1*st*, We find both *before* and under the *Law*
of *Moses* frequent Appearances not only of subordinate Angels, but even of the *great Angel*,
the *Logos* himself, in *humane Form* : this is an
evident *negative* Proof that Vehicles or Bodies
are *not unsuitable* to any subordinate Spiritual
Beings : and when it is farther consider'd that
the *Logos*, who is the first and highest *deriv'd*
Agent, not only took a *Body* of *Flesh* and so
was made *Man* ; but in the same humane Nature and Body is exalted to the most perfect
state of Glory and Happiness ; and advanc'd to
higher Degrees of Knowledge and Power in a
humane Body, than any Angel or Spiritual Being is ; this shews that the Union of a *material*
Body is not only *not unsuitable*, but is perfectly
consistent with the Nature of the most perfect
deriv'd Agent ; and capable of adding Encrease
of Glory and Happiness to that Being, who, be-

fore

fore he took it, was in the *Form of God, the Image of the invisible God*, the *First-born*, and constituted the *Head, of every Creature*. For the raising Christ's *Body* from the dead, and exalting it to the right Hand of God, and of Heavenly Majesty and Power, was the *Reward* of his Sufferings ; and that *Joy*, for the prospect of which *he endur'd the Cross, despising the shame of it :* and therefore the Union of the humane Body to the Person of Christ cannot but be thought most suitable to the Dignity and Felicity of the highest heavenly State. And if a Body be most suitable to an Agent of so great Dignity and Perfection, it cannot be suppos'd to be less suitable to Beings or Agents of an inferior Nature.

2*dly* ; In relation to ourselves we find, even in this imperfect state of Union with a *gross, earthly* Body, the Soul to exert in some Persons very great and surprizing Degrees of *Intelligence* ; and we not only cannot conceive *how* we shou'd be able to exert our Spiritual Faculties without the assistance of *Matter* ; but are assur'd from divine Revelation that we shall not enjoy that full and complete state of Happiness which God has prepar'd for them that *love him, without Bodies* ; and that they shall rise in a glorious Condition, to enable us to take possession and render us capable of it : and that in this state of our *glorified Bodies* we shall be *like unto the Angels* ; perhaps in bodily Form as well as in Glory and Happiness : for we cannot conceive any more suitable to the highest Perfection than

an

an *humane* Form, fince Chri*ſ*t himſelf enthron'd
in Heaven is inveſted with it. And 'tis not
improbable that as ourSouls have their firſt ſtate
of Exiſtence in *Body*, ſo they never are deſtitute
of one; or mere *naked Spirits*; but at the ſe-
paration of them from this *Earthly Tabernacle*,
they have a *Clothing* or *Body* from *Heaven*, ſome
Vehicle or other wherein to live and act in the
intermediate ſtate. I cannot ſay I have inter-
preted St. *Paul's* meaning in that difficult Place,
2 *Cor.* 5. 2, 4. but I think the Thing itſelf is
not improbable. And it was only the Conſideration of ſuch *heavy, groſs, ſluggiſh* Bodies as
we now have, which made the old *Pythagorean*
and *Platonic* Philoſophers think they were giv-
en us as *Priſons* and *Puniſhments* to our Souls
for Sins committed in a ſtate of pre-exiſtence to
them; and that it was abſurd and unſuitable
to a ſtate of Happineſs to have them rais'd from
the dead: for at the ſame time they thought
that all Souls in the ſtate of their pre-exiſtence
to the fleſhly Body, had *material, aerial,* or
cœleſtial Forms or Vehicles to which they were
united; and that they retain'd theſe Forms after the Death of the Fleſhly Body, which ob-
ſcur'd and reſtrain'd the Vigour and Activity of
them: and that even their *Dæmons* and *cœleſtial
mediatorial Gods* were all inveſted with ſhining,
ætherial Bodies: and probably St. *Paul* had an
eye to theſe Opinions, when he deſcrib'd the
Bodies of the Saints riſing in a *glorious* and *immortal* State.

Hence

Hence we may more clearly underftand the *Nature* and *Greatnefs* of the Punifhment pronounc'd by God on the Tranfgreffion of our firft Parents [and which thro' them equally affects all Mankind, one or two excepted] when he made the Death of the *Body* the Penalty of their Difobedience. This we cannot conceive to have been a *real* Punifhment, if the *Soul* in the feparate and invifible ftate cou'd *exift* and *act* as well and live as *happily* without it as with it. If the Soul when reconcil'd to God by *Repentance* [which his Goodnefs always difpos'd him to accept] cou'd exift in as perfect a ftate without a Body as with one ; then it is plain that the Threatning and Execution of Death upon the Body had no real Terror or Punifhment in it. But if our Souls (as we have Reafon to believe) are fo fram'd, as not to be naturally capable of fo much Happinefs without the Union of a Body to them, as in a ftate of Union with Body ; the *Punifhment* of Sin by the Diffolution of the Body is very apparent ; and the Redemption from this Punifhment by the *Refurrection* of a *glorious* and *incorruptible* Body, inftead of a *grofs, corruptible* one, muft be a great Mercy and Reward ; and worthy of the *Son of God* himfelf to come down from Heaven, and to take a *Body prepar'd for him*, both to qualify us for an happy Refurrection, by teaching and engaging us to do the Will of God reveal'd by him to us ; and alfo to give us an example of it by the Refurrection of his own Body from the dead to a moft glorious and heavenly ftate.

What

What care God takes of the Souls of the righteous who died in a ſtate of Repentance before the coming of Chriſt, or ſince the Terms of Reconcilement were propos'd and a Covenant of Grace thro' Faith in him hath been eſtabliſh'd with all Mankind who are call'd to this Faith, we cannot certainly tell : but 'tis probable that ſince *all live unto him,* and *with him,* they have (as I obſerv'd) *material* Vehicles inſtead of their Bodies, wherein to *act* and *live,* till the Time for the Redemption of their Bodies from Corruption ſhall be fulfill'd. And 'tis alſo probable, that as the *Souls* of the *Righteous* will gain great Advancements of Bliſs and Perfection by the Reunion of their Bodies rais'd to a glorious, *incorruptible* ſtate, which without them they cou'd not be naturally capable of ; ſo the *Souls* of the *Wicked* will undergo greater Degrees of Miſery and Puniſhment by the Reunion of their Bodies rais'd to an *inglorious* ſtate, than they otherwiſe are naturally capable of.

Laſtly ; The true Reaſon why the *Supreme, Self-exiſtent* God cannot be *incarnate,* or united to any *Material* Body, is the *Eſſential Infinity* of his Nature [for which Cauſe alſo he is *abſolutely inviſible*] whereby he is neceſſarily *preſent* to all Things *equally* ; and the *Eſſential Activeneſs* of it, whereby 'tis impoſſible that *his Perſon* ſhou'd ever by any Union with Matter become *acted upon* or *paſſive :* and it is moſt reaſonable to think that as all created Beings are neceſſarily *paſſive* or capable of being *acted upon,* ſo the Exiſtence of the intelligent

Part

Part of all such Beings united to Matter is determin'd and circumscrib'd by it : and therefore probably no created Agent hath much Extension.

And as God *knows every Thing* and *acts every where*, by being *Essentially* and *Substantially* present to all Things; so all other intelligent Agents know only by the Exercise of their intelligent Part on Objects receiv'd from External Things, to which Objects they are immediately present, or by *Revelation* from God, by what means soever it is made to them; and act in Places where they are not Substantially or Personally present, by the *Ministry* of other Agents who are put in Subordination to them.

Hence, as the *Holy Ghost* acts by the *Will* of God in subordination to Christ in the Affairs of his Church or Spiritual Kingdom ; so 'tis probable that Myriads of *Angels* [who are made subject unto Christ and said to *minister to those who shall be Heirs of Salvation*] act in subordination to *Him* for the good Government and Accomplishment of the *Kingdom of Christ*.

F I N I S.